ATLANTIS

ALSO BY MARK DOTY

My Alexandria (1993)

Bethlehem in Broad Daylight (1991)

Turtle, Swan (1987)

MARK DOTY

ATLANTIS

POEMS

HarperPerennial

A Division of HarperCollins*Publishers*

Grateful acknowledgment to the editors of the following magazines, in which these poems first appeared, sometimes in earlier versions: *The American Voice*, "Michael's Dream"; *The Atlantic*, "A Display of Mackerel," "Long Point Light"; *Art and Understanding*, Part 2 of "Fog Argument"; *Boulevard*, "Grosse Fuge"; *Carolina Quarterly*, "Migratory," "March"; *Columbia*, "Two Ruined Boats"; *Cosmos*, "In the Community Garden"; *Defined Providence*, "Couture," "Wreck"; *Folio*, Part 1 of "Fog Argument"; *The Georgia Review*, "Four Cut Sunflowers, One Upside Down"; *Global City Review*, "Crêpe de Chine"; *Indiana Review*, "To the Storm God"; *The Nation*, "Atlantis"; *The New Yorker*, "Coastal," "A Green Crab's Shell," "Tunnel Music"; *Parnassus*, "Nocturne in Black and Gold"; *PN Review*, "Aubade: Opal and Silver," "A Letter from the Coast"; *Phoebe*, "Two Cities"; *Witness*, "Homo Will Not Inherit"; *The Yale Review*, "Description."

"Rope" and "A Letter from the Coast" appeared in *A Place Apart: A Cape Cod Reader* (Norton, 1993). "Description" appeared in *Sanctuary, the Journal of the Massachusetts Audubon Society*.

My gratitude, as well, to the John Simon Guggenheim Memorial Foundation, the Ingram Merrill Foundation, and the Massachusetts Cultural Council for their generous support, and to Michael Carter, Jane Cooper, Ruth Doty, Jean Valentine, and David Wojahn for their irreplaceable help with this book.

FIRST EDITION

Designed by Alma Hochhauser Orenstein

ISBN 0-06-055362-6/ISBN 0-06-095106-0 (pbk.)

95 96 97 98 99 ❖/HC 10 9 8 7 6 5 4 3 2 1
95 96 97 98 99 ❖/HC 10 9 8 7 6 5 4 3 2 1 (pbk.)

for Wally

What more is there to love than I have loved?
And if there be nothing more, O bright, O bright . . .

WALLACE STEVENS

∾ CONTENTS

～ Description

My salt marsh
—mine, I call it, because
these day-hammered fields

of dazzled horizontals
undulate, summers,
inside me and out—

how can I say what it is?
Sea lavender shivers
over the tidewater steel.

A million minnows ally
with their million shadows
(lucky we'll never need

to know whose is whose).
The bud of storm loosens:
watered paint poured

dark blue onto the edge
of the page. Haloed grasses,
gilt shadow-edged body of dune. . .

I could go on like this.
I love the language
of the day's ten thousand aspects,

the creases and flecks
in the map, these
brilliant gouaches.

But I'm not so sure it's true,
what I was taught, that *through*
the particular's the way

to the universal:
what I need to tell is
swell and curve, shift

and blur of boundary,
tremble and spilling over,
a heady purity distilled

from detail. A metaphor, then:
in this tourist town,
the retail legions purvey

the far-flung world's
bangles: brilliance of Nepal
and Mozambique, any place

where cheap labor braids
or burnishes or hammers
found stuff into jewelry's

lush grammar,
a whole vocabulary
of ornament: copper and lacquer,

shells and seeds from backwaters
with fragrant names, millefiori
milled into African beads, Mexican abalone,

camelbone and tin, cinnabar
and verdigris, silver,
black onyx, coral,

gold: one vast conjugation
of the verb
to shine.

And that
is the marsh essence—
all the hoarded riches

of the world held
and rivering, a gleam
awakened and doubled

by water, flashing
off the bowing of the grass.
Jewelry, tides, language:

things that shine.
What is description, after all,
but encoded desire?

And if we *say*
the marsh, if we forge
terms for it, then isn't it

contained in us,
a little,
the brightness?

∾ Four Cut Sunflowers, One Upside Down

Turbulent stasis on a blue ground.

What is any art but static flame?
Fire of spun gold, grain.

This brilliant flickering's

arrested by named (Naples,
chrome, cadmium) and nameless

yellows, tawny golds. Look

at the ochre sprawl—*how*
they sprawl, these odalisques,

withering coronas
around the seedheads' intricate precision.

Even drying, the petals curling
into licks of fire,

they're haloed in the pure rush of light
yellow is. One theory of color,

before Newton broke the world
through the prism's planes

and nailed the primaries to the wheel,
posited that everything's made of yellow

and blue—coastal colors
which engender, in their coupling,

every other hue, so that the world's
an elaborated dialogue

between citron and Prussian blue.
They are a whole summer to themselves.

They are a nocturne
in argent and gold, and they burn

with the ferocity
of dying (which is to say, the luminosity

of what's living *hardest*). Is it a human soul
the painter's poured

into them—thin, beleaguered old word,
but what else to call it?

Evening is overtaking them.
In this last light they are voracious.

∾ A Green Crab's Shell

Not, exactly, green:
closer to bronze
preserved in kind brine,

something retrieved
from a Greco-Roman wreck,
patinated and oddly

muscular. We cannot
know what his fantastic
legs were like—

though evidence
suggests eight
complexly folded

scuttling works
of armament, crowned
by the foreclaws'

gesture of menace
and power. A gull's
gobbled the center,

leaving this chamber
—size of a demitasse—
open to reveal

a shocking, Giotto blue.
Though it smells
of seaweed and ruin,

this little traveling case
comes with such lavish lining!
Imagine breathing

surrounded by
the brilliant rinse
of summer's firmament.

What color is
the underside of skin?
Not so bad, to die,

if we could be opened
into *this*—
if the smallest chambers

of ourselves,
similarly,
revealed some sky.

～ Rope

Our street unspools toward the harbor,
    swerving past guesthouses,
the ancient jumble of roses,
    fencepickets in a formal tumble
crowded as a Persian miniature:
    a crazy quilt,

every corner filled. Where there might
    be a vacant spot there's a boat
in drydock—*Clorox*, unfortunate moniker—
    and an intricate strip of garden
where someone's knotted a tapestry
    of kale and sweetpeas

beside a roped pyramid of lobster traps.
    It's the first place
I've ever really wanted to live.
    Art, Milton Avery wrote,
is turning a corner; you don't know
    what's around the bend

till you go there. Our curve
    surprises with harbor glitter:
a bobbing dinghy, a sunstruck triangle
    of boats, two trawlers
idly going about whatever
    their business is. . .

Here, just where the street bends
    is my favorite house: shingled, narrow,
an elaborate Edwardian toaster

of a house, covered with moss
and drifting, almost perceptibly,
    towards collapse.

Antony lives there, and Charley.
    They walk early or late
to escape the heat; Charley,
    the antique spaniel, on his rope leash,
so much time elapsed between steps
    you might take him

for porcelain, an incredibly decrepit
    Staffordshire figurine,
or a particularly far gone carpetbag
    of buffalo hide, something allowed
to molder in a heap in the barn until mice
    made of it

their own version of the granaries
    of Babylon. He is that old.
I don't know if Antony would move faster
    on his own—I've never seen him
without Charley—but his pace
    precisely matches

his dog's, as if together they were
    one thing (something submarine,
adapted to the pressure of great depths).
    I've seen them down on the shore
in the evening, leaning against the shoulder
    of an upturned dory;

"We're soaking up some moonshine,"
    Antony calls. The truth is
I avoid them, since Antony delivers monologues
    which do not have endings—lucid,

interesting even, but listening's
        a commitment of uncertain,

considerable length. I don't see them
        for days, and then I worry,
since you can almost smell
        the fragility of their age,
 and when Charley cries a little,
        from the difficulty

of picking himself up on those
        no longer reliable legs,
Antony cannot hear him.
        I am a little surprised,
every time they reappear,
        and glad. They stand for hope,

and seem as tentative and constant
        as the steeple of the Unitarian church,
which leans a little to the right,
        but stands. Lately Charley
is not walking well; a few steps
        and those legs buckle

beneath him, so Antony has constructed
        a sort of rope harness,
which the good soldier of ongoingness
        wears, and when he falls
and looks up from those droozed,
        ancient eyes,

which have seen the rise
        of empires, from which the face
has sagged away, relinquishing

its form to the steady pull
of earth, Antony can lift him
    up again,

even hold him suspended
    a while, so that Charley
can move his failing legs
    and feel that he has been
for a walk. The neighbors say,
    When that dog goes . . .

But who'd suggest Charley's lived
    long enough? Think of Solomon,
who commanded the child be divided
    between mothers; who could cut apart
one living thing, or sever the rope
    that holds them both

in the world? It's frayed as it is.
    Art is this strong,
exactly: love's gravity,
    the weight of Charley's body,
in his rope harness, suspended
    from his master's hand.

∿ A Display of Mackerel

They lie in parallel rows,
on ice, head to tail,
each a foot of luminosity

barred with black bands,
which divide the scales'
radiant sections

like seams of lead
in a Tiffany window.
Iridescent, watery

prismatics: think abalone,
the wildly rainbowed
mirror of a soapbubble sphere,

think sun on gasoline.
Splendor, and splendor,
and not a one in any way

distinguished from the other
—nothing about them
of individuality. Instead

they're *all* exact expressions
of the one soul,
each a perfect fulfilment

of heaven's template,
mackerel essence. As if,
after a lifetime arriving

at this enameling, the jeweler's
made uncountable examples,
each as intricate

in its oily fabulation
as the one before
Suppose we could iridesce,

like these, and lose ourselves
entirely in the universe
of shimmer—would you want

to be yourself only,
unduplicatable, doomed
to be lost? They'd prefer,

plainly, to be flashing participants,
multitudinous. Even now
they seem to be bolting

forward, heedless of stasis.
They don't care they're dead
and nearly frozen,

just as, presumably,
they didn't care that they were living:
all, all for all,

the rainbowed school
and its acres of brilliant classrooms,
in which no verb is singular,

or every one is. How happy they seem,
even on ice, to be together, selfless,
which is the price of gleaming.

~ Couture

Peony silks,
      in wax-light:
            that petal-sheen,

gold or apricot or rose
      candled into—
            what to call it,

lumina, aurora, aureole?
      About gowns,
            the Old Masters,

were they ever wrong?
      This penitent Magdalen's
            wrapped in a yellow

so voluptuous
      she seems to wear
            all she's renounced;

this boy angel
      isn't touching the ground,
            but his billow

of yardage refers
      not to heaven
            but to pleasure's

textures, the tactile
        sheers and voiles
              and tulles

which weren't made
        to adorn the soul.
              Eternity's plainly nude;

the naked here and now
        longs for a little
              dressing up. And though

they *seem* to prefer
        the invisible, every saint
              in the gallery

flaunts an improbable
        tumble of drapery,
              a nearly audible liquidity

(bright brass embroidery,
        satin's violin-sheen)
              raveled around the body's

plain prose: exquisite
        (dis?)guises: poetry,
              music, clothes.

2.

Nothing *needs* to be this lavish.
        Even the words I'd choose
            for these leaves:

intricate, stippled, foxed,
          tortoise, mottled, splotched
                    —jeweled adjectives

for a forest by Fabergé,
          all cloisonné and enamel,
                    a yellow grove golden

in its gleaming couture,
          brass buttons
                    tumbling to the floor.

Who's it for?
          Who's the audience
                    for this bravura?

Maybe the world's
          just *trompe l'oeil*,
                    appearances laid out

to dazzle the eye;
          who could see through *this*
                    to any world beyond forms?

Maybe the costume's
          the whole show,
                    all of revelation

we'll be offered.
          So? Show me what's not
                    a world of appearances.

Autumn's a grand old drag
          in torched and tumbled chiffon
                    striking her weary pose.

Talk about your mellow
        fruitfulness! Smoky alto,
                thou hast thy music,

too: unforgettable,
        those October damasks,
                the dazzling kimono

worn, dishabille,
        uncountable curtain calls
                in these footlights'

dusky, flattering rose.
        The world's made fabulous
                by fabulous clothes.

∿ Grosse Fuge

                  This October morning,
soft lavender bursts above the Plymouth
parked on the neighbors' lawn: lilacs, wildly
off schedule, decking themselves a second time.
Downtown, on the Universalist green,
the chestnuts drop their sleek mahogany
under lanterned branches, tallowy blooms:
season of contradictions, tempest-wrought.
Summer's hurricane battered each branch bare,
skies suddenly wider, space in heaven
opened, our garden scoured as if by frost.
The little stars' jewel fires more consuming.
That was August, but all at once we wanted
to unpack sweaters, wrap ourselves in warm,
saturated tones: gems and harvest, moss.
But when real autumn came, the calendar
down to its last, late pages, the world
displayed its strange dependability
in disarray, rekindling: crocus
quickened, spiking through the fallen leaves,
then cherry and box-alder budded out,
and now this rash, breathtakingly sudden
bloom.
                  Bobby arrives on a Saturday,
and sits on the end of the couch, scarlet
parka and a red Jamaican hat fished
from the closet pulled tight. Why's he so cold?
This false spring? No, he looks—how to say it?
—small, not just his circumstances but *him*
somehow reduced. His landlord doesn't want
him back, his sister's dropped him on the side

20

of the highway, at a rest stop, his clothes
in three flowered yellow pillowcases.
My mother, he says, *doesn't want me*
crying in the house; she doesn't want
my tears around. She fed him on paper plates,
kept his laundry separate and didn't tell
his father the diagnosis. We say
of course he can stay and Sunday he wakes
saying, *I have four things inside me:*
a backyard going around and around
in my head this way, lawn furniture
spinning the other way, and right here,
in my chest, chairs. It's not that they hurt,
it's that I can't figure how I'm going
to get them the fuck out. He never says just what
the fourth thing is.
                        This month the new comes
so dizzyingly quick it coexists
with all autumn's evidence: by the marsh,
the usual sumptuous russets, sparked
by pointillist asters. Rugosas dot
the goldenrods' velveteen. Tulips sprout,
the crab leafs out. How are we to read
this nameless season—renewal, promise,
confusion? Should we be glad or terrified
at how quickly things are replaced?
Never again the particulars
of that August garden: waving cosmos,
each form's crisp darkness in relief
against the stars. No way to *know* what's gone,
only the new flowerings, the brilliance
that candles after rain; every day
assuming its position in the huge
gorgeous hurry of budding and decline:
bloom against dry leaf, unreconciled sorts
of evidence.

I have been teaching myself
to listen to Beethoven, or trying to—
learning to *hear* the late quartets: how hard
it is, to apprehend something so large
in scale and yet so minutely detailed.
Like trying to familiarize yourself,
exactly, with the side of a mountain:
this birch, this rock-pool, this square mosaic
yard of tesserated leaves, autumnal,
a jeweled reliquary. Trying to see
each element of the mountain and then
through them, the whole, since music is only
given to us in time, each phrase parcelled
out, in time.
          Thursday he says *All night*
I had to make Elizabeth Taylor's
wedding cake. It was a huge cake,
with nine towers, all of them spurting
like fountains, and she didn't like it,
and I had to make it again, then
the thing was it wasn't really a cake
anymore.
          I am trying to understand
the *Grosse Fuge*, though I'm not sure what
it might mean to "understand" this stream
of theme and reiteration, statement
and return. What does it mean, chaos
gathered into a sudden bronze sweetness,
an October flourish, and then that moment
denied, turned acid, disassembling,
questioned, rephrased?
          MRI: charcoaled flowers,
soft smudges, the image that is Bobby,
or Bobby's head, or rather a specific
plane bisecting his head pictured on video,
cinematic, rich inky blacks, threaded

by filaments and clouds. I stand behind
the door, and watch the apparition
taking form beyond the silhouette
of the technician who wore gloves to touch him
(fully clothed, dry, harmless, but the coward
wrapped himself in latex charms anyway,
to ward off the black angel). On the screen,
like a game, he makes a Bobby of light,
numbers, and images—imagines?—Bobby
as atoms of hydrogen, magnetic,
aligned, so that radio waves transmitted
toward the body bounce back, broadcasting
this coal-smudged sketch: brain floating
on its thick stem, and little strokes of dark
everywhere, an image I can't read,
and wasn't supposed to see—but who could
stay away from the door? Which of these
darknesses, if any, is the one which
makes his bed swim all night with boxes,
insistent forms, repeated, rearranged?
In one of those, he says, *is the virus,*
a box of AIDS. And if I open it . . .

I bring home, from each walk to town, pockets
full of chestnuts, and fill a porcelain
bowl with their ruddy, seducing music
—something like cellos, something that banks deep
inside the body. The chestnuts seem lit
from within, almost as if by lamplight,
and burnished to warm leather, the color
of old harnesses . . .
                    I have four bottles,
cut glass cologne bottles, right here, under
my ribs, by my heart. Can you tell the doctor?
I can't, he doesn't like me.

Scribbled notes,
Opus 130: first movement: everything
rises to this sweetness, each previous note
placed now in context, completed, once
the new phrase blooms. Second movement: presto,
skittering summation of the first.
Next, andante broken open
by the force of feeling it contains,
tumbling out into moments of intense
punctuation, like blazing sumac,
goldenrod so densely interwoven
in the field I can't keep any of it
separate for long: pattern of cadence,
spilling out, forward, then cessations.
Like seeing, in jeweled precision,
exact, wet and startlingly *there*, oak leaves,
and birch, and exclamations of maple:
the flecked details of the piebald world.
Seeing it all, taking it in, and yet
rising up to see at once whole forests . . .
Is that it? All my work of listening,
and have I only learned that Beethoven
could see the forest *and* the trees?
                    Bobby
cries on the couch: *All I want is one head.*
Later, *My head and my legs are one thing.*
Over breakfast: *Please, you've got to tell me,*
the truth now, no matter what, swear.
The boxes, do they ever hold still?
They're driving me crazy with their dancing.
Mostly he looks away, mouth open,
as if studying something slightly above
and to the right of the world.
                         The music
is like lying down in that light which gleams
out of chestnuts, the glow of oiled and rubbed

mahogany, of burled walnut, bird's-eye
maple polished into incandescence:
autumn's essence of brass and resin, bronze
and apples, the evanescent's brisk smoke.
But how is a quartet—abstract thing—
passionate, autumnal, fitful, gleaming,
regretful, hesitant, authoritative,
true? Is any listening an act
of translation, a shift of languages?
Even the music words themselves may make?
Flutter of pendant birch. Then I pull
myself back from the place where the music
has brought me; the music is not leaves,
music is not Bobby's illness; music,
itself, is always *structure*: redolent,
suggestive occasion, a sort of scaffold
which supports the branching of attention.

After the flood of detail the quartet
conjures, nothing: the great block of silence
which the fugue has defined around itself.
When I was seventeen, and everyone
I knew acquired a new vocabulary—*mantra*,
sutra, *Upanishads*—I learned a chant,
in Sanskrit, *gātē gātē pārāgātē*
is all I can remember of the words
but the translation goes *gone gone beyond*
gone, altogether beyond gone, and that
is where the music has gone, and Bobby's
going,
          though not today, not yet. AZT's
a toxic, limited miracle, and
Bobby's in the kitchen, banging
the teakettle, cursing the oatmeal,
the first time he's been up in weeks. Last night,
when a Supremes song graced the radio,

he suddenly rose, coiffed in his blanket,
and lip-synched twenty seconds of blessed,
familiar drag routine. He's well enough
to be a bitch, to want a haircut
and a shave. Still too sick to go home,
—wherever that might be—and too ill, as well,
to stay: the truth is we can't live
in such radical proximity to his dying.
But not today. In the wet black yard,
October lilacs. Misplaced fever? False flowering,
into the absence the storm supplied?
Flower of the world's beautiful will
to fill, fill space, always to take up space,
hold a place for the possible? A little
flourish, a false spring? What can I do but echo
myself, vary and repeat? Where can the poem end?
What can you expect, in a world that blooms
and freezes all at once?
There is no resolution in the fugue.

~ At the Boatyard

What I love at the boatyard,
at the end of Good Templar Place,
is the scraped, accidental intensity

of color. How could intention ever match
the mottled peacock of the Paolo Marc,
scrubbed to unforgettable azure?

Two of the racks of pink
paint-flecked spars
are empty, this morning,

but the third holds the lavender,
milky, rust-blurred bulk
of the Carla Bee, out of Boston

—long out of Boston, I'd say,
from the way her ancient propeller
is bearded, Confucian.

The same spars held,
just yesterday, the wire-brushed green
of a hull named Dora.

Dora! Green peeled to blue
then cloudy red then
the original green still staining

the steamed wooden arc:
fabulous tones, glazed
to transparency by saltwater.

I think that green
is what I've wanted
all my life: uncompromised,

warmed in the March sun
here where the sheds provide
a little shelter,

at the juncture of elements.
A pair of rusty tracks
curve up out of the harbor—

a railway arriving from the bottom
of the sea? This border
between worlds is dotted

with planks and buckets and ropes
but sinuous still as any wilder coast,
and the drowned boat off the pier

is every day more waterlogged,
less salvageable; it glows,
in the weak sun, apricot.

No one hauls her up
to the emptied cradles
which have sent their work

back into the harbor
stripped and buffed
and shining. And some days,

only when I am not looking,
a slick brother head
watches from between the lapping,

mirror waves. He is whiskered,
placid, and keeps his distance,
lone ambassador

of the marine. He lives
in some darker gradation
of that desired green—oh,

who knows how he lives?
And if the self is half-submerged,
gone in that watery, other element,

might not the secretive swimmer
be befriended? My sleek double
chucks his marvelous head and dives.

～ A Letter from the Coast

All afternoon the town readied for storm,
    men in the harbor shallows hauling in small boats
        that rise and fall on the tide. Pleasure,

one by our house is called. I didn't think
    the single man who tugged her in could manage
        alone, though he pushed her up high enough,

he must have hoped, to miss the evening's
    predicted weather: a huge freight of rain
        tumbling up the coast. There's another storm

in town, too, a veritable cyclone
    of gowns and wigs: men in dresses here for a week
        of living the dream of crossing over.

All afternoon they braved the avenue
    fronting the harbor, hats set against the wind,
        veils seedpearled with the first rain,

accessoried to the nines. The wardrobes
    in their rented rooms must glitter,
        opened at twilight when they dress

for the evening, sequin shimmer
    leaping out of the darkness . . . Their secret's
        visible here, public, as so many are,

and in that raw weather I loved
    the flash of red excess, the cocktail dress
        and fur hat, the sheer pleasure

of stockings and gloves.
     I'm writing to tell you this:
          what was left of the hurricane arrived by ten.

All night I heard, under the steep-pitched shallows
     of our sleep, the shoulders of the sea flashing,
          loaded, silvering with so much broken cargo:

shell and rusted metal, crabclaw and spine,
     kelp and feathers and the horseshoe carapace,
          and threading through it all the foghorns'

double harmony of warning, one note layered
     just over and just after the other. *Safety,*
          they said, or *shelter,* two inexact syllables

repeated precisely all night, glinting
     through my dream the way the estuaries
          shone before sunup, endless

invitation and promise, till dawn
     beat the whole harbor to pewter.
          Pleasure was unmoved and burnished a cobalt

the exact shade of a mussel's hinge,
     and every metal shone in the sea: platinum,
          sterling, tarnished chrome.

The law of the tide is accumulation, *More,*
     and our days here are layered detail,
          the shore's grand mosaic of detritus:

tumbled beach glass, endless bits
     of broken china, as if whole nineteenth-century kitchens
          went down in the harbor and lie scattered

at our feet, the tesserae of Byzantium.
    Those syllables sounded all night,
        their meaning neither completed nor exhausted.

What was it I meant to tell you?
    All I meant to do this storm-rinsed morning,
        which has gone brilliant and uncomplicated

as silk, that same watery sheen?
    How the shore's a huge armoire
        full of gowns, all its drawers packed

and gleaming? Something about pleasure
    and excess: thousands of foamy veils,
        a tidal wrack of emerald, glamor

of froth-decked, dashed pearl bits.
    A million earrings rinsed in the dawn.
        I wish you were here.

~ To the Storm God

Our single local houseboat,
the morning after the storm,
lies on its side on the shore,

awkward, elephantine,
splotched, on its green bottom,
with broad red strokes of paint,

almost a hexagram—no,
too scattered. This beached glyph
is unreadable,

bold de Kooning gestures
on an emerald field.
It was a pelting storm,

the air throbbing with pulses
of rain, the bay frothing;
the floating house was only

a room built atop a boat, square,
like a city apartment.
Unballasted, its four walls

caught every scrap of wind;
I'd seen it spinning in the bay
all season, careening in breezes

too weak to lift a kite.
Who could live there, or sleep
in that tossing, homemade craft,

too wildly buffeted
by even the smallest wave
to free the dreamer

from the waking life?
Just down the beach,
a dinghy called the Ciao Bella

—the little boat of our neighbor,
the restaurateur—has landed
high on shore, splayed

like a crisp red and white
hors d'oeuvre, centerpiece
of some fabulous antipasto.

The green plank seats
stretch above a contained ocean:
inside the hull

a little sand, rippling water,
a garland of sea lettuce
and—look!—a dozen yellow-eyed minnows

thread the bright ripples
like a pack of embroidery needles
on amphetamines. Startled,

they hide from my shadow
under the shadow of a plank.
Boat become home

for the houseless fishes,
houseboat become the fishes' home;
daily the world mounts

such reversals, brews tempests,
confounds elements—containing
the uncontainable sea,

smashing open the containing house.
I love the wet ideograms
scrawling the houseboat

—great wrecked heart—
its underlife enormous now,
incontrovertible. The minnows

fill the firmament
of the Ciao Bella, this watery isle
they inhabit for today;

let me live in these estuaries'
blue and salt edges, washed
in the headlong currents

that rise beneath sleep
and spill into the day
like tidewash, mist

out of nowhere veiling
the day-lashed harbors
in uncertain or rapturous light.

Turn me in any wind, go ahead,
break my house apart.
How else could I learn to read

the characters scrawling
this houseboat's revealed canvas,
how else would I learn to say them?

∾ In the Community Garden

It's almost over now,
late summer's accomplishment,
and I can stand face to face

with this music,
eye to seed-paved eye
with the sunflowers' architecture:

such muscular leaves,
the thick stems' surge.
Though some are still

shiningly confident,
others can barely
hold their heads up;

their great leaves wrap the stalks
like lowered shields. This one
shrugs its shoulders;

this one's in a rush
to be nothing but form.
Even at their zenith,

you could see beneath the gold
the end they'd come to.
So what's the use of elegy?

If their work
is this skyrocket passage
through the world,

is it mine to lament them?
Do you think they'd want
to bloom forever?

It's the trajectory they desire—
believe me, they do
desire, you could say they are

one intent, finally,
to be this leaping
green, this bronze haze

bending down. How could they stand
apart from themselves
and regret their passing,

when they are a field
of lifting and bowing faces,
faces ringed in flames?

∽ Breakwater

After the crowded houses disperse,
after the bleached condos
of the summer millionaires
accentuating the beach

like stress marks pencilled
on a line of verse, after the squared lawns
and hedges watered into emerald,
and the final, fascist architecture

of the motel, suddenly,
uninterrupted horizon: a long exhalation
of marsh greening out to
—there, that far white line,

salt or spume or dune
disturbed, sometimes, by hurrying
Euclidian sails, or the whale watch boat
chugging its load out to hover

over the feeding depths.
Here, curving out to the farthest reaches,
the breakwater's a causeway of huge stones.
Hard to think these were *placed*,

these drowsy, inland boulders
awakened, all century, by the seawater's
moon-driven alarm. Who piled them,
one atop the other,

into this enormous arc?
It seems impractical:
a simple straight line
could shield the shellfish fields

and erasable dunes. Instead,
this great stone eyebrow
raised above the bay; fluid,
slim curve slung across the hard glint

of radiance this morning, and yesterday
into the smudged pastels
of fog. Toward—what?
I have been to the end, once:

after the casual walkers turn back,
after the few fishermen cast
their vanishing silvery hopes
across the acid gardens of sea lettuce,

the stonework's rough and tumble,
less neatly arrayed, and thick
with the bleached wicker of tidewrack
where gulls leave the shattered evidence

of mussels. Either because you must
concentrate on your footing,
or because the curve's so subtle,
you hardly know you are turning

until you're at the marshy, other end,
where eelgrass scribbles the boundary
between bay and shore, and sea lavender
bursts in little violet explosions

over the shivering water.
No one's there. Or almost no one—
I saw three ducks, poised in a kind of Chinese stasis.
A solitary hiker, resting

on the lee side of the stones,
read a novel, the solid book positioned
comfortably between himself and the landscape.
I envied him, a little, the heavy,

absorbing certainties of his book,
his carefully directed attention.
There was so much to see,
and at the same time so strangely little:

the world reduced to elemental,
almost abstracted planes of color and light.
How much further could there be to go?
Here, one turns around—and there's

the same line arcing back to land, glorious,
undisturbed by having been traversed.
An architecture—no, more pure,
the sheer principle of curve:

the flaring, imagined shape
between then and now,
now and the future, a flung
silken gesture made into the space

between reader and book,
uncertainty and knowledge.
We did not know we had come so far.
What did you see along the way?

Flowers and stones, strangers and books,
water and light . . . That path
looked so different, so particular,
while we were travelers, and it arcs,

now that we have come to rest,
as mysteriously as ever,
as nearly perfect a shape
as ever we'll discern.

~ Long Point Light

Long Point's apparitional
   this warm spring morning,
      the strand a blur of sandy light,

and the square white
   of the lighthouse—separated from us
      by the bay's ultramarine

as if it were nowhere
   we could ever go—gleams
      like a tower's ghost, hazing

into the rinsed blue of March,
   our last outpost in the huge
      indetermination of sea.

It seems cheerful enough,
   in the strengthening sunlight,
      fixed point accompanying our walk

along the shore. Sometimes I think
   it's the where-we-will-be,
      only not yet, like some visible outcropping

of the afterlife. In the dark
   its deeper invitations emerge:
      green witness at night's end,

flickering margin of horizon,
   marker of safety and limit.
      But limitless, the way it calls us,

and where it seems to want us
  to come. And so I invite it
    into the poem, to speak,

and the lighthouse says:
  Here is the world you asked for,
    gorgeous and opportune,

here is nine o'clock, harbor-wide,
  and a glinting code: promise and warning.
    The morning's the size of heaven.

What will you do with it?

~ Atlantis

1. FAITH

        "I've been having these
awful dreams, each a little different,
though the core's the same—

we're walking in a field,
Wally and Arden and I, a stretch of grass
with a highway running beside it,

or a path in the woods that opens
onto a road. Everything's fine,
then the dog sprints ahead of us,

excited; we're calling but
he's racing down a scent and doesn't hear us,
and that's when he goes

onto the highway. I don't want to describe it.
Sometimes it's brutal and over,
and others he's struck and takes off

so we don't know where he is
or how bad. This wakes me
every night now, and I stay awake;

I'm afraid if I sleep I'll go back
into the dream. It's been six months,
almost exactly, since the doctor wrote

not even a real word
but an acronym, a vacant
four-letter cipher

that draws meanings into itself,
reconstitutes the world.
We tried to say it was just

a word; we tried to admit
it had power and thus to nullify it
by means of our acknowledgement.

I know the current wisdom:
bright hope, the power of wishing you're well.
He's just so tired, though nothing

shows in any tests, Nothing,
the doctor says, detectable;
the doctor doesn't hear what I do,

that trickling, steadily rising nothing
that makes him sleep all day,
vanish into fever's tranced afternoons,

and I swear sometimes
when I put my head to his chest
I can hear the virus humming

like a refrigerator.
Which is what makes me think
you can take your positive attitude

and go straight to hell.
We don't have a future,
we have a dog.
                    Who is he?

Soul without speech,
sheer, tireless faith,
he is that-which-goes-forward,

black muzzle, black paws
scouting what's ahead;
he is where we'll be hit first,

he's the part of us
that's going to get it.
I'm hardly awake on our morning walk

—always just me and Arden now—
and sometimes I am still
in the thrall of the dream,

which is why, when he took a step onto Commercial
before I'd looked both ways,
I screamed his name and grabbed his collar.

And there I was on my knees,
both arms around his neck
and nothing coming,

and when I looked into that bewildered face
I realized I didn't know what it was
I was shouting at,

I didn't know who I was trying to protect."

2. REPRIEVE

I woke in the night
and thought, *It was a dream,*

nothing has torn the future apart,
we have not lived years

in dread, it never happened,
I dreamed it all. And then

there was this sensation of terrific pressure
lifting, as if I were rising

in one of those old diving bells,
lightening, unburdening. I didn't know

how heavy my life had become—so much fear,
so little knowledge. It was like

being young again, but I understood
how light I was, how without encumbrance,—

and so I felt both young and awake,
which I never felt

when I *was* young. The curtains moved
—it was still summer, all the windows open—

and I thought, I can move that easily.
I thought my dream had lasted for years,

a decade, a dream can seem like that,
I thought, *There's so much more time . . .*

And then of course the truth
came floating back to me.

You know how children
love to end stories they tell

by saying, It was all a dream? Years ago,
when I taught kids to write,

I used to tell them this ending spoiled things,
explaining and dismissing

what had come before. Now I know
how wise they were, to prefer

that gesture of closure,
their stories rounded not with a sleep

but a waking. What other gift
comes close to a reprieve?

This was the dream that Wally told me:
I was in the tunnel, he said,

and there really was a light at the end,
and a great being standing in the light.

His arms were full of people, men and women,
but his proportions were all just right—I mean

he was the size of you or me.
And the people said, Come with us,

we're going dancing. And they seemed so glad
to be going, and so glad to have me

join them, but I said,
I'm not ready yet. I didn't know what to do,

when he finished,
except hold the relentless

weight of him, I didn't know
what to say except, *It was a dream,*

nothing's wrong now,
it was only a dream.

3. MICHAEL'S DREAM

Michael writes to tell me his dream:
I was helping Randy out of bed,
supporting him on one side
with another friend on the other,

and as we stood him up, he stepped out
of the body I was holding and became
a shining body, brilliant light
held in the form I first knew him in.

This is what I imagine will happen,
the spirit's release. Michael,
when we support our friends,
one of us on either side, our arms

under the man or woman's arms,
what is it we're holding? Vessel,
shadow, hurrying light? All those years
I made love to a man without thinking

how little his body had to do with me;
now, diminished, he's never been so plainly
himself—remote and unguarded,
an otherness I can't know

the first thing about. I said,
You need to drink more water
or you're going to turn into
an old dry leaf. And he said,

Maybe I want to be an old leaf.
In the dream Randy's leaping into
the future, and still here; Michael's holding him
and releasing at once. Just as Steve's

holding Jerry, though he's already gone,
Marie holding John, gone, Maggie holding
her John, gone, Carlos and Darren
holding another Michael, gone,

and I'm holding Wally, who's going.
Where isn't the question,
though we think it is;
we don't even know where the living are,

in this raddled and unraveling "here."
What is the body? Rain on a window,
a clear movement over whose gaze?
Husk, leaf, little boat of paper

and wood to mark the speed of the stream?
Randy and Jerry, Michael and Wally
and John: lucky we don't have to know
what something is in order to hold it.

4. ATLANTIS

I thought your illness a kind of solvent
dissolving the future a little at a time;

I didn't understand what's to come
was always just a glimmer

up ahead, veiled like the marsh
gone under its tidal sheet

of mildly rippling aluminum.
What these salt distances were

is also where they're going:
from blankly silvered span

toward specificity: the curve
of certain brave islands of grass,

temporary shoulder-wide rivers
where herons ply their twin trades

of study and desire. I've seen
two white emissaries unfold

like heaven's linen, untouched,
enormous, a fluid exhalation. Early spring,

too cold yet for green, too early
for the tumble and wrack of last season

to be anything but promise,
but there in the air was white tulip,

marvel, triumph of all flowering, the soul
lifted up, if we could still believe

in the soul, after so much diminishment . . .
Breath, from the unpromising waters,

up, across the pond and the two-lane highway,
pure purpose, over the dune,

gone. Tomorrow's unreadable
as this shining acreage;

the future's nothing
but this moment's gleaming rim.

Now the tide's begun
its clockwork turn, pouring,

in the day's hourglass,
toward the other side of the world,

and our dependable marsh reappears
—emptied of that starched and angular grace

that spirited the ether, lessened,
but here. And our ongoingness,

what there'll be of us? Look,
love, the lost world

rising from the waters again:
our continent, where it always was,

emerging from the half-light, unforgettable,
drenched, unchanged.

5. COASTAL

Cold April and the neighbor girl
    —our plumber's daughter—
        comes up the wet street

from the harbor carrying,
    in a nest she's made
        of her pink parka,

a loon. *It's so sick,*
    she says when I ask.
        Foolish kid,

does she think she can keep
    this emissary of air?
        Is it trust or illness

that allows the head
    —sleek tulip—to bow
        on its bent stem

across her arm?
    Look at the steady,
        quiet eye. She is carrying

the bird back from indifference,
    from the coast
        of whatever rearrangement

the elements intend,
    and the loon allows her.
        She is going to call

the Center for Coastal Studies,
   and will swaddle the bird
      in her petal-bright coat

until they come.
   She cradles the wild form.
      Stubborn girl.

6. NEW DOG

Jimi and Tony
can't keep Dino,
their cocker spaniel;
Tony's too sick,
the daily walks
more pressure
than pleasure,
one more obligation
that can't be met.

And though we already
have a dog, Wally
wants to adopt,
wants something small
and golden to sleep
next to him and
lick his face.
He's paralyzed now
from the waist down,

whatever's ruining him
moving upward, and
we don't know
how much longer
he'll be able to pet
a dog. How many men
want another attachment,
just as they're
leaving the world?

Wally sits up nights
and says, *I'd like
some lizards, a talking bird,
some fish. A little rat.*

So after I drive
to Jimi and Tony's
in the Village and they
meet me at the door and say,
We can't go through with it,

we can't give up our dog,
I drive to the shelter
—just to look—and there
is Beau: bounding and
practically boundless,
one brass concatenation
of tongue and tail,
unmediated energy,
too big, wild,

perfect. He not only
licks Wally's face
but bathes every
irreplaceable inch
of his head, and though
Wally can no longer
feed himself he can lift
his hand, and bring it
to rest on the rough gilt

flanks when they are,
for a moment, still.
I have never seen a touch
so deliberate.
It isn't about grasping;
the hand itself seems
almost blurred now,
softened, though
tentative only

because so much will
must be summoned,
such attention brought
to the work—which is all
he is now, this gesture
toward the restless splendor,
the unruly, the golden,
the animal, the new.

～ Two Cities

I awoke in Manhattan, just after dawn,
in the tunnels approaching Grand Central:
a few haunted lamps, unreadable signs.

And with a thousand others,
each of us fixed on the fixed point
of our destination, whatever

connection awaited us, I spilled
up the ramp and under the vault
and lugged my bag out onto 42nd Street,

looking for the Carey bus.
What had I been dreaming?
I had grown sick of human works,

sum and expression of failure; spoilers,
brutalizers of animals and of one another,
self-absorbed until we couldn't see

that we ruined, finally, ourselves
—what could we make? The epidemic unhalted,
the ill circumscribed, worthless;

the promises hollow, the poor and marginal
hopelessly and endlessly marginal and poor.
This steeping ink colored everything,

until I felt surrounded by weakness
and limit, and my own energies failed,
or were failing, though I tried

not to think so. Dawn was angling into the city;
smoky, thumb-smudged gold struck first
a face, not human, terracotta,

on an office building's intricate portico,
seeming to fire the material from within,
so that the skin was kindled,

glowing. And then I looked up:
the ramparts of Park Avenue were radiant,
barbaric; they were continuous

with every city's dream
of itself, the made world's
angled assault on heaven.

Manhattan was one splendidly lit idea,
its promises held in a disturbed,
golden suspension. Weeks later,

there was a second city,
not really a city at all:
nights, in the coastal town

where I live, voices, engines
cough over the water
from the pier where trawlers cluster

and fog-pearled lamps
shimmer the undulant harbor,
so that wharf's end

becomes a distant city, foreign,
storied: extended downward
in the flung glitter of reflection

(as if it floated, on pylons of light,
above a gilt, Oriental double,
domes and towers blurred by rising smokes)

and radiating upward, also, above itself,
in mist's ethereal wash—a Venice,
a city dreaming itself into being?

Had I walked out there,
as I do, some nights,
I wouldn't have reached it;

that capital's coherent
only from this distance,
a fable built and erased

and drawn again
as surely as Manhattan is.
"Venice," Nietzsche said,

"is a city of a hundred solitudes."
New York is a city of ten million,
and my American Venice—liquid avenues,

phantom boulevards rippling
and doubled in the dark—a city
of two hundred and fifty million

solitaires, the restless dreamers'
dreamed magnificence: our longing's
troubled mirror, vaporous capitol.

∾ Tunnel Music

Times Square, the shuttle's quick chrome
flies open and the whole car floods with
—what is it? Infernal industry, the tunnels
under Manhattan broken into hell at last?

Guttural churr and whistle and grind
of the engines that spin the poles?
Enormous racket, ungodly. What it is
is percussion: nine black guys

with nine lovely and previously unimagined
constructions of metal ripped and mauled,
welded and oiled: scoured chemical drums,
torched rims, unnameable disks of chrome.

Artifacts of wreck? The end of industry?
A century's failures reworked, bent,
hammered out, struck till their shimmying
tumbles and ricochets from tile walls:

anything dinged, busted or dumped
can be beaten till it sings.
A kind of ghostly joy in it, though
this music's almost unrecognizable,

so utterly of the coming world it is.

∾ Crêpe de Chine

These drugstore windows
—one frame in the mile-long film
of lit-up trash and nothing

fronting the avenue, what Balzac called
"the great poem of display"—
are a tableau of huge bottles

of perfume, unbuyable gallons of scent
for women enormous as the movie screens
of my childhood. Spiritual pharmaceuticals

in their deco bottles,
wide-shouldered, flared,
arrayed in their pastel skylines,

their chrome-topped tiers:
a little Manhattan of tinted alcohols.
Only reading their names

—Mme. Rochas, White Shoulders, Crêpe de Chine—
and I'm hearing the suss of immense stockings,
whispery static of chiffon stoles

on powdered shoulders,
click of compacts, lisp and soft glide
of blush. And I'm thinking of my wig,

my blonde wig, and following the cold sparkle
of pavement I'm wanting not
these shoes but the black clatter

and covenant of heels. Next door
the Italian baker's hung a canopy of garlands
and silver shot, bee lights and silk ivy

high over the sugary excess
of his pastries, and I want
not his product but his display:

I want to wear it,
I want to put the whole big thing
on my head, I want

the tumbling coiffeurs of heaven,
or lacking that, a wig
tiered and stunning as this island.

That's what I want from the city:
to wear it.
That's what drag is: a city

to cover our nakedness,
silk boulevards, sleek avenues
of organza, the budding trees

along the avenue flaunting their haze
of poisonous Caravaggio green. . .
Look how I take the little florists' shops

and twist them into something
for my hair, forced spiky branches
and a thousand tulips. Look, my sleety veil

of urbane rain descends, unrolls
like cinema's dart and flicker, my skirt
in its ravaged sleekness, the shadows

between buildings raked and angled
into these startling pleats,
descending twilight's gabardine

over the little parks and squares
circled by taxis' hot jewels:
my body

made harmonious with downtown.
Look how I rhyme with the skyscraper's
padded sawtooth shoulders,

look at the secret evidence of my slip
frothing like the derelict river
where the piers used to be,

look at my demolished silhouette,
my gone and reconstructed profile,
look at me built and rebuilt,

torn down to make way,
excavated, trumped up, tricked out,
done, darling,

in every sense of the word. Now,
you call me
Evening in Paris, call me Shalimar,

call me Crêpe de Chine.

∼ Migratory

Near evening, in Fairhaven, Massachusetts,
seventeen wild geese arrowed the ashen blue
over the Wal-Mart and the Blockbuster Video,

and I was up there, somewhere between the asphalt
and their clear dominion—not in the parking lot,
its tallowy circles just appearing,

the shopping carts shining, from above,
like little scraps of foil. Their eyes
held me there, the unfailing gaze

of those who know how to fly in formation,
wing-tip to wing-tip, safe, fearless.
And the convex glamor of their eyes carried

the parking lot, the wet field
troubled with muffler shops
and stoplights, the arc of highway

and its exits, one shattered farmhouse
with its failing barn . . . The wind
a few hundred feet above the grass

erases the mechanical noises, everything;
nothing but their breathing
and the perfect rowing of the pinions,

and then, out of that long, percussive pour
toward what they are most certain of,
comes their—question, is it?

Assertion, prayer, aria—as delivered
by something too compelled in its passage
to sing? A hoarse and unwieldy music

which plays nonetheless down the length
of me until I am involved in their flight,
the unyielding necessity of it, as they literally

rise above, ineluctable, heedless,
needing nothing . . . Only animals
make me believe in God now

—so little between spirit and skin,
any gesture so entirely themselves.
But I wasn't with them,

as they headed toward Acushnet
and New Bedford, of course I wasn't,
though I was not exactly in the parking lot

either, where the cars nudged in and out
of their slots, each taking the place another
had abandoned, so that no space, no desire

would remain unfilled. I wasn't there.
I was so filled with longing
—is that what that sound is for?—

I seemed to be nowhere at all.

⮁ Homo Will Not Inherit

Downtown anywhere and between the roil
of bathhouse steam—up there the linens of joy
and shame must be laundered again and again,

all night—downtown anywhere
and between the column of feathering steam
unknotting itself thirty feet above the avenue's

shimmered azaleas of gasoline,
between the steam and the ruin
of the Cinema Paree (marquee advertising

its own milky vacancy, broken showcases sealed,
ticketbooth a hostage wrapped in tape
and black plastic, captive in this zone

of blackfronted bars and bookstores
where there's nothing to read
but longing's repetitive texts,

where desire's unpoliced, or nearly so)
someone's posted a xeroxed headshot
of Jesus: permed, blonde, blurred at the edges

as though photographed through a greasy lens,
and inked beside him, in marker strokes:
HOMO WILL NOT INHERIT. *Repent & be saved.*

I'll tell you what I'll inherit: the margins
which have always been mine, downtown after hours
when there's nothing left to buy,

the dreaming shops turned in on themselves,
seamless, intent on the perfection of display,
the bodegas and offices lined up, impenetrable:

edges no one wants, no one's watching. Though
the borders of this shadow-zone (mirror and dream
of the shattered streets around it) are chartered

by the police, and they are required,
some nights, to redefine them. But not now, at twilight,
permission's descending hour, early winter darkness

pillared by smoldering plumes. The public city's
ledgered and locked, but the secret city's boundless;
from which do these tumbling towers arise?

I'll tell you what I'll inherit: steam,
and the blinding symmetry of some towering man,
fifteen minutes of forgetfulness incarnate.

I've seen flame flicker around the edges of the body,
pentecostal, evidence of inhabitation.
And I have been possessed of the god myself,

I have been the temporary apparition
salving another, I have been his visitation, I say it
without arrogance, I have been an angel

for minutes at a time, and I have for hours
believed—without judgement, without condemnation—
that in each body, however obscured or recast,

is the divine body—common, habitable—
the way in a field of sunflowers
you can see every bloom's

the multiple expression
of a single shining idea,
which is the face hammered into joy.

I'll tell you what I'll inherit:
stupidity, erasure, exile
inside the chalked lines of the police,

who must resemble what they punish,
the exile you require of me,
you who's posted this invitation

to a heaven nobody wants.
You who must be patrolled,
who adore constraint, I'll tell you

what I'll inherit, not your pallid temple
but a real palace, the anticipated
and actual memory, the moment flooded

by skin and the knowledge of it,
the gesture and its description
—do I need to say it?—

the flesh *and* the word. And I'll tell you,
you who can't wait to abandon your body,
what you want me to, maybe something

like you've imagined, a dirty story:
Years ago, in the baths,
a man walked into the steam,

the gorgeous deep indigo of him gleaming,
solid tight flanks, the intricately ridged abdomen—
and after he invited me to his room,

nudging his key toward me,
as if perhaps I spoke another tongue
and required the plainest of gestures,

after we'd been, you understand,
worshipping a while in his church,
he said to me, *I'm going to punish your mouth*.

I can't tell you what that did to me.
My shame was redeemed then;
I won't need to burn in the afterlife.

It wasn't that he hurt me,
more than that: the spirit's transactions
are enacted now, here—no one needs

your eternity. This failing city's
radiant as any we'll ever know,
paved with oily rainbow, charred gates

jeweled with tags, swoops of letters
over letters, indecipherable as anything
written by desire. I'm not ashamed

to love Babylon's scrawl. How could I be?
It's written on my face as much as on
these walls. This city's inescapable,

gorgeous, and on fire. I have my kingdom.

❧ Fog Argument

1. JADE

Of course I know it ends.
I know there's a precise limit

where salt marsh gives way
to fogged water's steel.

But from here, from moor's edge
where the tide pond

doubles the swallows,
it doesn't seem to;

blonde acres
vanish at the rim

into the void,
a page on which anything

might be written,
though nothing is. What I love

is trying to see
the furthest grassy extreme,

that fog-marbled horizontal. . .
Rippling strokes, a few high dunes

hung on the edges of the page
like Chinese brushstrokes,

barely there, and out
on the far shore

the sea gone a clouded mint,
gone without edges, horizon erased,

a single silken exhalation
the color of mown grass,

unripe persimmon, gooseberry,
juniper, sage, green shadow

in the hollow of collarbone,
love, I know, it ends,

you don't have to remind me,
though it seems a field

of endless jade.

2. BEACH ROSES

What are they, the white roses,
when they are almost nothing,
only a little denser than the fog,

shadow-centered petals blurring,
toward the edges, into everything?

This morning one broken cloud
built an archipelago,
                    fourteen gleaming islands

hurrying across a blank plain of sheen:
nothing, or next to nothing

—pure scattering, light on light,
fleeting.
            And now, a heap of roses
beside the sea, white rugosa
beside the foaming hem of shore:
                              brave,
waxen candles . . .

                And we talk
as if death were a line to be crossed.
Look at them, the white roses.
Tell me where they end.

～ Wreck

This drowned trawler's
　　rested comfortably
　　　　on the tide flats for years,

filled and emptied
　　like some legendary storehouse.
　　　　High tide, up close,

you can see from the wharf
　　red portholes looming up—
　　　　windows observing us

from another, less mortal element?
　　It's the shadowy heart,
　　　　today, of a triangle

of white boats, sun-lashed
　　and nodding; its broken profile
　　　　lends depth to their lightness,

substance to their grace.
　　This boat's pickled in salt,
　　　　but preserved, I think,

by sheer persistence;
　　some things have such a will
　　　　to be themselves

they don't take to decay,
　　even wave-beaten and scoured
　　　　by seekers of salvage

and souvenir. I love this evidence.
    Ghost, it is more stubborn
        than live things. Ruin,

it lasts, though the bay's
    huge indifference laves what might,
        should, at any moment, cave in,

dissolve—what must, in any tempest,
    scatter the shore in unrecognizable
        fragments. It doesn't, hasn't,

I want to say won't:
    something must hold,
        some chambered wreck

must fill and empty daily,
    seawater pouring like the future
        —I need this evidence—

into the hulk which admits
    and releases and keeps
        its grip on the shore.

~ Two Ruined Boats

Here, at the edge of immensity,
they seem the axis of the harbor,
my twin derelicts, destinations
of every morning's walk, center

of a composition made vaster
by the startling appearance of sun,
this first day of spring, on snow
the tide is busily erasing. First,

the Sarah Lynn (she was called
something else once, another name
looming beneath peeling letters,
unreadable palimpsest). Look

at the sheer intricacy of wreck,
somber, self-shadowing; how many colors
rust is, all vaguely luminous,
like fifty shades of eyeshadow.

This drenched failure suggests
a whole aesthetic of ruin: salt patinas,
flecked and scoured exactitudes,
a history of color: Venetian reds,

brazilwood, cochineal. Here, *morello*,
the color of ripe Italian blackberries,
here the *berrettino* of raw silk.
And though it all seems to be

approaching dissolution, all going blank
as the dank interior glimpsed
(chinablack, like antique ink)
through the shattered hatch,

how various and complicated
these frettings are en route
to nothing. The mast lies prone
across the sand, striped with yellow.

A hundred yards up the shore,
the Diane S. is optimistically propped
on the sand, though her underside's split out
like a tired accordion's. Dry,

upright, one side bleaches
to a lush indigo; the other's lustered
in crocus tones, layers and layers
the colors in old Woolworth's watercolor boxes.

Across the prow, a hand-lettered sign,
in jonquil: *Wanted: Artists actors
and musicians to restore the Diane S.
and sail to China.* I would, myself,

avoid that passage: this decline's
too steep to fix, and my art
could only articulate the sheen,
or chronicle the fashion in which

the world gains luster as it falls apart.
Besides, I like this inhospitable shore,
this coastal snow warmed, on shingled roofs,
to gleaming eggwhite. I don't need to go anywhere.

Description is itself a kind of travel,
and I can study all day in an orient
of color. A ruin in shadow and a ruin in sun,
a light-shivered companion

and another which hurries inward
toward whatever looms in the hull's
blank interior. Two ruined boats
—like myself, my lover,

twin points we thought fixed
coming all undone, though in flaring spring sun
the world's a single dazzled silver.
That's all I can do, describe.

I've nowhere else to go, nothing else
to make. This poem's a distillation
of a thousand morning walks,
and by the time I wrote this down,

in truth, my twin tokens,
my brave figures of persistence
were swept clear away,
some misguided civic gesture

to make the beach a cleaner place.
I didn't know it was coming.
Who ever does? Who'd have thought
those grand lexicons of color would be

hammered by the backhoe to wrack and powder?
Fallen down, broken apart, carried away:
things are lovely, late, in the last hour
we'll see them. This year? Next month?

I watch him failing and there's nothing to do
but describe—a mode of travel,
but not a means of repair.
That morning, on Pearl Street,

beneath the thin spray of sand
a town truck had sown,
the pavement shone like a mackerel's back,
and slick puddles marbled our reflections

(old red coat, sleek black dog tending slightly
to the portly) until they were refracted
and reassembled, melting in—what would you call
this color?—gorgeous disarray.

～ March

*"I'm so lucky!" my lover said to me again and again in the last
year of his life.*

FENTON JOHNSON, "THE WEIGHT OF MEMORY"

I thought the choice was to love austerity
or not to love at all,

but when I went out to look at the elemental
I found nothing sparse, only this density

and saturation: dusky sedge
at the pond's rim, thicket and tumble

of violet contradiction, plum stems—
a whole vocabulary of tone and hue, demanding,

a history steeped in the long practice
of luminosity. How difficult

just to say what's here, in March severity.
Try. The sky's

a complicated scheme, in grisaille,
the sort of vault that used to host

rings of saints around the rim
of heaven. From the footbridge

the pond's scoured stainless; wind-driven,
aluminum water shivers and unwrinkles

just above the ice, a steely sheet
interrupted by fountaining grass.

Lichen-maps on the beeches,
banks stippled in sullen milky greens,

and out on the ice a dozen gulls pose
for Whistler, a composition in twenty aspects

of gray: severe music, something atonal,
Japanese? And though the world's locked

in sere, pilgrim winter, look: transparence,
depth. Here, in lustrous sedges,

at pond's edge, in violet tumbling thicket,
nothing spare: the subtlest

dazzlings, progressions of argent
and indigo. Even, in the mosses,

summer's deep watered greens,
verdigrised copper, grazed and cropped

chartreuse fixed and fired here
in the cold, the world's glazes embedded

and swirled, arcs of pigment on marbled paper:
frozen, galactic, held.

Nocturne in Black and Gold

Shadow is the queen of colors.
ST. AUGUSTINE

Tonight the harbor's
    one lustrous wall, the air a warm gray
        —mourning dove, moleskin, gabardine—

blurring the bay's black unguent.
    And, gradually, a few light patches
        —boats? ghosts of lamps

where the pier ends?
    The memory of lamps?
        In Whistler's "Nocturnes"

you can barely see
    the objects of perception,
        or rather there are no solids,

only fields of shimmer,
    fitful integers of gleam,
        traces of a rocket's shatter,

light troubling a shiver of light.
    Fogged channels, a phantom glow
        on the face of this harbor,

midway between form and void,
    without edges, hypnagogic.
        Listen, I carry myself

like a cigarette lighter
          wrapped between hands in the dark
                    and so feel at home in the huge

indefinition of fog, the same
          sort of billowing I am: charcoal, black on black,
                    matte on velveteen, a hurrying sheen

on gleaming docks. Keats: *If a sparrow*
          come before my Window
                    I take part in its existence

and pick about the Gravel.
          If we're only volatile essence,
                    permeable, leaking out,

pouring into any vessel bright enough
          to lure us, why be afraid?
                    Having been a thousand things,

why not be endless?
          Act II, *Die Zauberflöte*:
                    the Queen of the Night

ascends her lunar glissando,
          soprano cascading upward
                    until you'd swear

this isn't a voice at all;
          she's become an instrument,
                    an instant's pure

erasure, essence slipped
          into this florid scatter:
                    rhinestones shivering

on a tray lacquered black
        with coldest ozone. *Königin,*
                Königin der Nacht:

chill shine, icy traces . . .
        Here, at wharf's end,
                the trawlers' winking candles

all undone, phantom girandoles
        nearly extinguished
                by the cool salve

of fog. Haven't we wanted,
        all along, to try on boundlessness
                like mutable, starry clothes?

Isn't it a pleasure,
        finally, to be vaporous,
                to be cloudy flares

like these blurred lamps,
        ready to shift or disperse
                or thin to a glaze of atmosphere,

sheer, rarefied, without limit?
        Königin der Nacht: that dizzying pour
                is a voice becoming no one's,

one empty glove
        brushing the evening's cold cheek
                like the clear exhalation

of a star. Against the firmament's
        gleaming patent,
                the Queen's voice

no longer even human:
      a gilt thread raveling
            in the dark. How lucky,

vanishing, to become *that*,
      at once evanescent
           and indelible. Love,

little pilot flame, flickering,
      listen: I've been no one
           so many times I'm not the least afraid.

Doesn't everything rush
      to be something else?
           Won't it be like this,

where you're going: shore and bay,
      harbor and heaven one continuum
           sans coast or margins?

No one's here,
      or hardly anyone, and how strangely
           free and fine it is

to be laved and extended, furthered
      in darkness, while shadows
           give way to other shadows,

and the bay murmurs
      its claim: *You're a rippling,*
           that quick, and you long to be

loose as air again, unfettered
      freshness, atmosphere
           and aria, an aspect of fog,

manifest, and then dissolving,
        which you could regret
                no more than fog.

A brave candling theory
        I'm making for you,
                little lamplight, believe,

and ripple out free
        as shimmer is. Go.
                Don't go. Go.

~ Aubade: Opal and Silver

First snow, unrolling scrim, my dogs running
through a continuously descending voile

of little white darts, heaven's
heavy silver blushed to lavender

at the rim: what opera is this,
the curtain falling all morning,

its figured ripple airy and endless?

Two hurriers, just after dawn,
one black and one golden: the new dog,

the one my lover's asked for
in the last month of his life

racing unbridled now, abandoning himself
to the arc of his transit

through these brilliant strokes
crosshatching the bay's pewter.

First snow, opal and silver,
evidence and demonstration:

from the magician's secret wardrobes
emerge whole realms of costume,

not one of them ever worn twice.
Here's enough antique lace

to sew a bodice for the harbor,
its silver-skinned breathing

dotted now with little flowers of ice.

Here a dreaming princess decked
in forty bolts of eyelet,

a wicked mandarin whose lunar silks
are flecked with ashen butterflies:

apparitions of time—who'll play,
and wreck, each character in the comedy.

That's the nature of the trick:
time animates what it kills.

Two arcs, one black and one golden,
racing ahead till they're only

quick strokes on the page
the shore's become, under a sky

intimate and iridescent
as the interior of a gem. Time's

not the enemy, nothing
as simple as that; our old enchanter

—dressmaker to reality—

works these fierce and delicate effects
from somewhere in the wings.

From nowhere, shifting tableaux
—for our instruction

and delight? meant to confound us?—
come looming through the morning's

steadily unfolding screen,
the silken undulation

between this life and the next,
now and *ever*. A lip of sun

—unpredictable appearance—
and the snowy billow's overshot

with gold like Favrile glass; this fabric's
spun of such insubstantial stuff

it doesn't quite conceal the other world.
Can't we see into it already, a little? Look,

there: two gestures, one black
and one golden, racing into the veil.

"Four Cut Sunflowers, One Upside Down" is titled after van Gogh; both this poem and "Two Ruined Boats" are indebted to Manlio Brusatin's *The History of Colors.*

"Grosse Fuge" is for Robert Shore, 1948–1993.

"A Letter from the Coast" is for Lynda Hull, 1954–1994.

"Breakwater" is for Herbert Morris.

The section of "Atlantis" entitled "Michael's Dream" is for Michael Trombley, Stephen Housewright, Maggie Valentine, Carlos Melendez, and Marie Howe. The section entitled "Coastal" is for Darren Otto.

"Tunnel Music" is for Philip Levine.

"Migratory" is after Hayden Carruth's "No Matter What, After All, and That Beautiful Word So."

"Homo Will Not Inherit" is for Michael Carter.

"Nocturne in Black and Gold" is titled after Whistler.

"Aubade: Opal and Silver," also titled after Whistler, is for Rena Blauner.

As well as for Wally Roberts (1951–1994), this book is for the many people, more than I can name, who helped to carry him during the last year of his life. O *World, I cannot hold thee close enough.*

MARK DOTY is the author of three previous collections of poems: *Turtle, Swan, Bethlehem in Broad Daylight,* and *My Alexandria.* He is the recipient of many awards for his work, including the National Book Critics Circle Award, the *Los Angeles Times* Book Award, a Whiting Writer's Award, and grants from the National Endowment for the Arts, the Guggenheim and Ingram Merrill Foundations, and the Massachusetts Cultural Council. He has taught at Sarah Lawrence College, Brandeis University, and the University of Iowa Writers Workshop. He lives in Provincetown, Massachusetts.